CROWNED
WITH
DAVID

40 Devotionals to Inspire Your Life,
Fuel Your Trust, and Help You Succeed
in God's Way

David Ramos

Thank You!

I appreciate you taking the time to check out my book. As a thank you, I would like to send you the gift *Dreaming with Joseph: 12 Devotionals to Inspire Your Faith, Encourage Your Heart, and Help Your Realize God's Plan.*

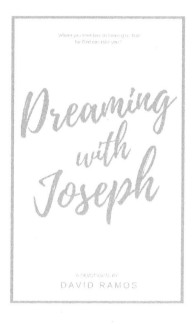

To claim your free copy simply go to RamosAuthor.com and enter your email address.

Table of Contents

Introduction

I have a special connection to the character of David since my parents chose to name me after him. Growing up, I heard the Bible stories time and time again about King David. His mighty rule, his incredible fighting power, and how God redeemed the mistakes he made.

David was larger than life to me – someone to look up to, someone to model my life after. If I was going to be *a* David, then I was going to become like *the* David. But somewhere along the line I stopped thinking like that.

David became a distant character. I had real, every day problems to deal with. How was I supposed to learn from someone who had never lived my life, never endured my troubles, never faced the disadvantages I faced? It was in the midst of this doubt and frustration that God took me into the Scriptures to see David in a whole new way.

At the deepest level, the story of King David is a story of trust. From the shepherd boy stuck in the fields of Bethlehem, to the conquering soldier, to the humiliated cheating murderer, and finally the greatest human King of Israel – in every instance, David had to learn to trust God in an intimate way.

David trusted God for his safety, for his forgiveness, and for his legacy. The story of David taught me that a life lived in the hands of God is indestructible.

What I want you to see over the next 40 days is the connection between trusting God and achieving greatness. David was obsessed with what God wanted. He fought and risked and took bold actions not because he was trying to make a name for himself, but because he wanted the name of God to be honored everywhere it was heard. David lived for a purpose bigger than himself and God used that devotion beautifully.

The success of our lives depends upon the worth of our focus. David lived an incomparable life because he never took his eyes off his incomparable God. I invite you now into the life of Israel's king, into this lesson of trust, and onto the path of being crowned with David…

The Ones God Chooses

The story of David begins in the shadow of Saul. Saul was the chosen king and he was everything the people hoped he would be...for a time. He was strong, attractive, and had the natural ability to lead. However, it was his gifts, in part, which led to his downfall.

Saul became obsessed with himself. He drifted from God and relied more and more upon his own strengths and abilities. Before long, Saul was no more than a tortured and angry soul. God turned his face away and told Samuel, the prophet of Israel, that it was time to choose another king.

Samuel feared for his life – anointing another king was amount to treason. Yet he obeyed and made his way to the city of Bethlehem. There, God brought before him a man named Jesse and his eight sons. One by one, Samuel observed each of them to see if they were who God had chosen to succeed Saul.

Samuel was looking for another strong leader. A man who could rouse the people to overcome Saul and follow God once again. But God was looking for something different, something less obvious.

"People look at the outward appearance, but the LORD looks at the heart."

Eventually, Jesse called for his youngest son. A small boy named David. As soon as Samuel saw David, he heard God speak, *this is the one.*

What do God's heroes look like? When we go to the movies or read stories, the heroes are always the ones who can do more. They have a special ability or a special story. Whether it's immense brainpower, super speed, or strong magic - each time we recognize who the hero is because of what they can do. But God's heroes are never those people.

He never chooses the ones everyone else would choose. He looks for the disadvantaged, the small, the scared, the unlearned and he transforms them into testimonies for His glory!

Apart from God, David was never going to be more than a shepherd. He was never going to slay giants or conquer armies until God pointed at him and said, *you are my chosen.*

God has done the same to you.

No matter the story you were born into or what struggles you have had, as soon as you let God take control of your life you become one of His chosen heroes. You become His anointed and He will take your life in a direction you could have never imagined.

Takeaway: God chooses the unlikely to do great things.

Prayer: Lord, thank You that You do not see as other people see. Please do something great with my life for Your glory.

Beyond Order

Day 2
1 Samuel 16:14-23

Once again the Bible shows how the stories of David and Saul are linked. Saul is in decline. The Lord has sent an evil spirit to torture him but Saul's attendants have an idea.

They want to bring someone who can play the lyre (a cross between a harp and a guitar) to help sooth Saul. The king agrees, and guess who is summoned to his court: David.

The move works. Saul finds peace whenever David plays and chooses to make him one of his armor-bearers, a prestigious role for someone so young and especially for an unknown shepherd boy.

Seemingly overnight, the boy who went unnoticed now held the attention of the king. How could this happen?

God plays by His own set of rules. When He decides to promote someone, He doesn't need to follow the logical order. He places people where

He desires and nothing on earth can stop Him.[i] So much of what we will see in David's story doesn't make sense because it isn't supposed to. A God-driven life is supposed to be strange. It's supposed to break rules and upend the normal order.

God told David that he would one day be king. David could have resigned to follow the normal path to get there. Perhaps he would have joined the army and proved he was a skilled warrior until they eventually promoted him. Decades would have went by and eventually he would have had enough support to make a claim to the throne. Hopefully by then, the king would have become unpopular or weak so that he could make his move.

But God circumvented all of that. He took the shepherd and placed him directly in the king's court. As we will see, he continued to show David favor and fast-tracked his story.

When God calls us to something we have two choices. We can either look for a way to make it happen in the natural or we can go towards the calling with complete abandon, knowing that if God promised it – He will be the One to make it happen.

Takeaway: God always delivers on His promises.

Prayer: Father, help me not to choose the safe path. Instead, push me to truly step in faith towards what You have put on my heart. I will trust You and I believe that You will do the rest.

Beyond Limits

Day 3
1 Samuel 17:1-33

David continued to be faithful where he was at, shepherding his father's flocks while his brothers went off to war against the Philistines. Little did David know, he would have a central role to play in the conflict.

Among the Philistines was a giant warrior named Goliath. He was fierce, intimidating, and above all an offensive creature. For forty days he mocked Israel and challenged their warriors to single combat. No one dared challenge him.

One day, Jesse sent David to deliver food to his brothers. On his way, David heard Goliath's rant against Israel. In that moment, the young man decided he would be the one to fight him.

Others discouraged David from taking on Goliath. First, his father Jesse kept him from the battles, making sheep his son's priority. Next, David's older brother Eliab yelled at him because he thought David had come to watch the battle and ignore his duties. Finally, Saul himself tried to deter David from fighting such an experienced warrior.

Again and again, people treated David according to the way he looked. He was young, untrained and inexperienced. Even more so, he was a fraction of Goliath's size. But none of that mattered because God was building something inside of him, something greater than his brothers, than Saul, and even greater than Goliath.

As servants of God, we are not bound by the limits other's place on us. People will always try to keep you from doing what they themselves are scared to do. Most of the time, their intentions are good and they only want the best life for you.

Yet over and over again the Scriptures show us that our best life is the one God has already planned. He will take us into frightening and dangerous places, not to harm us, but to mold us into the heroes He needs us to be.

So David prepared for battle, trusting that God would fight for him.

Takeaway: The life God has for us might contradict what our loved believe is best.

Prayer: God, I want to live the life You have planned for me. Help me not to be controlled by fear, but to trust in Your words above anyone else's.

Our Weakness, His Strength

Day 4
1 Samuel 17:34-54

The scene is set. Goliath, the champion of the Philistines, approaches in all his fury to battle the small challenger David. David, refusing to wear the bulky armor of Saul, enters the battlefield with only a slingshot, a few rocks, and his staff.

Everyone watching expected the worse. Here was this headstrong boy marching towards his suicide. They saw David's weaknesses, but God saw his faith.

Goliath yells, trying to intimidate David, proclaiming that he will give his flesh to animals today. But David does not back down. He yells back, *I come against you in the name of God, He is the one who fights for me, and it is your flesh the animals will eat today!*

Goliath charges at him, like an avalanche of metal. David readies his slingshot and before Goliath can ever lay a hand on the young boy, the rock crashes into his head sending him face first into the ground.

For good measure David then uses the giant's own sword to cut off his head. It's a brutal victory to say the least and we can only imagine the sense of awe that must have poured through the army of witnesses.

This story is very much symbolic of what God would do through Israel for generations to come.[ii] The nation of Israel, like David, was small. They were constantly surrounded by bigger, stronger enemies. Yet they won victory after victory.

God loves to choose the weak things, and help them overcome the strong.[iii] That's when His glory and power are most evident.

When God moves, He wants there to be no confusion about who was truly responsible. He chooses the frail, the poor, and the uneducated because then, when they do the impossible, there can be no other explanation than divine action.

You may feel like what God has called you to do is impossible. That you are the last person in the world qualified to serve Him in this way, but I assure you – that makes you His first choice. Because through your weakness, He will be shown as strong and able and good.

Takeaway: We should pursue the impossible because God's strength shows itself through our weakness.

Prayer: God Almighty, thank You that You choose the ones the world overlooks. Please give me the courage to do great things, and to let Your glory shine through me.

Proper Focus

Day 5
1 Samuel 18:5-16

After David's victory over Goliath, Saul chose to keep David in his service permanently. David did everything from playing the lyre to leading segments of the army for Saul. It wasn't long before all of Israel began to take notice of the young man's successes.

The people of Israel watched as David succeeded over and over again and honored him like they would a king. Saul became furious. Here was this young man stealing the favor of his people.

What was the cause behind David's meteoric rise? Verse 12 says it simply: "Saul was afraid of David, because the LORD was with David but had departed from Saul."

God was forcefully directing the events at this time. Whether David wants to or not, he was gaining immense popularity across the nation. At the same time, Saul's claim to the throne was diminishing. He was watching the kingdom he forged slip from his hands and everything he did seemed to work towards David's good.

Commentator McCarter Jr. adds this, "every action [Saul] takes relative to David contributes to his successes...everything [David] does, whether out of a desire for personal gain or not, brings him promotion and glory...both men are caught up in something larger than themselves, in events in which they must participate but cannot finally control."[iv]

When God wants something for your life there is no person or force on earth that can stop Him. David was not particularly ambitious at this stage in his life. He was still very young and above all, he wanted to please God. God loved David and took every opportunity to bless him as He paved the way for him to become king.

Once God has placed a calling on your life – something you know without a shadow of a doubt that He wants you to do, a task that you were specially created to complete – keep your eyes on Him and not that thing.

I believe one of the reasons David was so blessed during this time was because he was not trying to overthrow Saul and become king. His top concern was serving God and doing that by serving the king.

When we place more importance on fulfilling the call of God over having a relationship with God, that is when dangerous and painful things happen. God kept blessing David because he kept his eyes and heart towards Him. God left Saul for exactly the same reason – he chose to keep his eyes and heart on his own kingdom and away from God.

Takeaway: In our pursuit of great callings we will have to constantly ask ourselves: am I pursuing the thing more than God.

Prayer: Lord, my life is your vessel. Please direct my steps and keep my eyes and heart towards You. Help me to trust that You know what You are doing.

Trust and Freedom

Day 6
1 Samuel 18:20-27

As our story continues, Saul becomes increasingly desperate to get rid of David. He is watching this young man succeed in everything he does and it terrifies him. However, an opportunity arises.

Saul's daughter Michal loves David. And it's clear that David has feelings for her as well. Saul plans to use David's feelings against him and kill him in the process.

In this ancient context there was a *bride-price* associated with marriage. This was a sort of fee the man would pay to the woman's family in order to marry her, like a reverse dowry. Furthermore, the price was usually set by the status of the woman's family.[v] This is why David feels Michal is out of reach for him since he is "only a poor man and little known."

This is where Saul originates his plan. Instead of a monetary gift, he asks David to kill one hundred Philistines for him. To a normal man, this would have certainly meant death. But the Lord was with David, and he didn't only fulfill Saul's tall order – he doubled it, killing two hundred Philistines!

Saul saw David's victory and gave Michal to him as promised. The opportunity he thought would solve his problem only worked to add to his fears.

David was certainly an extraordinary figure, but he was still entirely human. His was a life touched by God's favor and grace. But it is important we remember something:

"no weapon forged against you will prevail...this is the heritage of the servants of the Lord" Isaiah 54:17

As servants of God we are undoubtedly going to face trials. People are going to want to watch us fall and cause us to get angry at God on the way down. However, we serve the same God as David.

I can't tell you that you will be protected from everything because life doesn't work like that (and growth does not come that way). What I can do is encourage you to live like David.

David set out against the Philistines without an ounce of doubt that he would be successful. It never crossed his mind that if God told him to do something, it might not be possible. How incredible would our journeys be if we believed in the same way?

What if we took God at His word and acted before we had all the details or covered all the bases? What would our lives look like if they were completely directed by the grace and power of God?

Takeaway: The more we trust God, the more freedom we will experience in our lives.

Prayer: Lord, forgive me for all the ways I refuse to trust you. I want to live a David-sized life. Help me trust You like he did.

Story Builders

Saul was on a dangerous downward spiral. In the text we have seen his character jump back and forth again and again when it comes to his feelings towards David. For a time, he loved the young man and brought him into his service. Now, Saul has struggled with the desire to kill David even though David has been nothing but good to him.

Saul's son, Jonathan, tries to intervene in this chapter. The two young men have become great friends. This bond was undoubtedly a breath of fresh air for David amidst all of the trials he has been through.

Jonathan was able to talk Saul out of killing David, at least for now. Everything seems calm until another war with the Philistines erupts. David rises to the challenge and gains victory, unintentionally stirring Saul's jealousy and anger once again.

When David returns to Saul, Saul attacks. He pulls out a spear and lunges it at David's body. Thankfully, David dodges the attack and flees the crazed king.

The people God chooses to place in our lives matter. God knew what he was doing by keeping Saul as king for a time and by having Saul's son, Jonathan, become friends with the future king.

People are one of the tools God uses to fulfill his promises upon the earth. He used Noah to restart his creation. He used Abraham to grow his chosen nation. And he used Jesus to seal salvation. God's stories always include people.

The same is true for your story. You may not be the chosen heir to a kingdom, but your story is no less important. When preparing Israel's new king, God did not just launch David into the spotlight. He used Samuel, Jonathan, Saul and many others to prepare the young man for his future.

Pay attention to the individuals God has placed in your life. They are there for a purpose. Even the ones who frustrate you. Each human is a color God is using to paint His masterpiece. We need others in order to live our best story, and they need you.

Takeaway: God does not work in a vacuum, He uses other people for our story.

Prayer: Father, thank you that you know why you created me. Please help me trust you with the relationships I have and help me to treasure them like I should.

Presence and Pain

Day 8
1 Samuel 19:11-24

David flees after Saul's attack and takes shelter with the prophet Samuel. The prophet's home, a place called Ramah, is very close to the capital so Saul quickly discovers where David has fled.

Saul is not going to let David get away this time. He immediately sends a group of soldiers to find and kill David. However, when the men arrive the "Sprit of God" comes upon them and they start to prophesy. During this, they are unable to attack David.

When news of what happened reaches Saul, he sends a second group. Again, the men are disarmed by the Spirit of God. Saul sends a third set only for them to fail one last time. Infuriated, Saul sets off to Ramah himself. He will be the one to kill David no matter what.

Before Saul even arrives to where Samuel and David are, the Spirit of God comes on him too and for the rest of the journey he prophesies as he discards his clothing. Saul found Samuel but was unable to do anything. God's spirit had disarmed him and caused him to lay naked for an entire day, giving Samuel and David time to escape to another place.

These verses present us with the scary reality of how far Saul has fallen. The man is overcome with bitterness and jealousy. He can no longer think clearly or lead justly. Saul is a shell of the man he was, but that is not even the worse part.

In this time, prophecy was seen as a gift. While there were a few who tried to take advantage of others through false words, those who truly had the gift were highly revered.

When Saul's soldiers came upon Ramah and began to prophesy, this would have been a good thing. They were experiencing a very rare gift from God. However, when Saul prophecies it is not seen as a good thing. Rather, God's presence has become a hazard to Saul's life: "The spirit of Yahweh now haunts [Saul] rather than helps him."[vi] The commentator goes on to say that this instance of prophecy was more like a disease given to Saul than a gift, and causes him to suffer deeply.

This is as far as a human can possibly fall. We were created to be near God. When God punished Adam and Eve for their sin, He cast them out of the garden because being away from

God was supposed to be the worst penalty. Here, Saul has encountered a new level of pain – where the presence of God, what we were created to experience, actually becomes the punishment.

Treasure the presence of God. Seek His voice, His word. Spend time wanting to know what God is really like. This what we were ultimately made for. When we forget, when we choose to treasure other things above God, that is when our purpose is at risk and the very thing we were meant to pursue becomes the thing we want to avoid.

Takeaway: God's presence can either be refreshing or frightening depending on the condition of our heart.

Prayer: God Almighty, forgive me for making lesser things more important than You. Help me not to be scared of Your presence but to want it more.

A Godward Friendship

Day 9
1 Samuel 20:1-42

After David's near brush with Saul, he flees to his friend Jonathan. Despite what Jonathan has seen of his father, and the fear in David's eyes, he does not believe that his father could really want to kill his best friend.

David and Jonathan come up with a plan. David will hide from Saul and miss the banquet that is about to happen. When Saul realizes that David is gone, if he remains calm then there is nothing to fear. However, if Saul gets angry that David is missing then Jonathan will know something is wrong.

The feast begins and before long, Saul notices David's absence. He asks Jonathan if he knows where David has gone, and he lies to protect his friend. Sure enough, Saul is overcome with anger and hurls a spear at his own son while cursing at him.

David was right. The two young men reunite, full of sadness and fear because the truth has just been made known. Jonathan and David make an oath to care for one another and their descendants. Afterward, David leaves for what might be the last time.

This is an emotional scene for many reasons. David is scared for his life. He is running out of people he can trust and now his best friend does not want to believe his story. Jonathan is caught in between his father and his friend and must choose a side.

For Jonathan, there is much more on the line than most readers realize. He was the eldest son of Saul and by law, the heir to his kingdom. By helping David, he was essentially giving away his right to become king one day.

This is a level of friendship far beyond what most of us will ever experience; true friendship – where one puts the concerns of others above themself. David did not have to convince Jonathan to do this. He did not have to sell him on the idea of him becoming king, or bargain with him to join his side over his father's.

When God is in control of our stories, he will guide the characters into their proper places. We do not have to try and control every element of our life when we are letting God direct our stories.

Takeaway: We will be amazed by what happens when we let go and let God.

Prayer: Father, help me to trust You more. I know you know what is best for my life and that You have more planned than I could ever imagine. My life is Yours.

Above It All

Day 10
1 Samuel 21:1-9

David escapes to a small place called Nob after his goodbye with Jonathan. The priest there is caught off guard. David was tantamount to a royal figure at this time. Showing up unannounced and without the royal guard would have been like the vice president coming to your house in dirty clothes and without the secret service.

David quickly creates a story to cover his appearance and explain the odd situation. The priest seems to buy it, at least for now. Next, a seemingly insignificant scene occurs.

David asks for bread but the only bread they have available is holy bread. This food was used for sacrifices and rituals and only after those were finished could the priests eat it. After a quick discussion about his purity, the priest gives David the bread to eat.

Why is this so important? There are two reasons: one having to do with David and the second having to do with Jesus.

David is fleeing for his life and clearly God is on his side. When Jonathan helped him in the previous chapter, it was symbolic of the "state" or government helping him. Now, when the priest feeds David, it's symbolic of the "church" helping him as well.[vii] God is not just moving small pieces around to prepare the way for David's kingship. He is bringing the most powerful institutions in the land under his feet in order to accomplish his plan.

If we fast-forward to Matthew 12, we see a similar scene where Jesus and his disciples eat grain from the field. When they are yelled at by the Pharisees, Jesus quotes this scene from David's story as justification.

There is nothing bigger than God. Every law, every structure, every roadblock must fall down to Him. This is the God David believed in and this is the God we serve. Jesus came and walked in the authority of his father in order to show us what was possible. Do not limit what God can do with your life and with your situation.

Takeaway: God is bigger than the big things that keep us from trusting Him.

Prayer: Thank You God for being Almighty. Help me believe that nothing can hinder Your good plans.

The Transforming Power of Trust

Day 11
1 Samuel 22:1-5

David is on the move once again. Much of David's story could be told through a map, tracing his route of escape from one chapter to the next. Here, David first runs to Adullam. From there, he seeks protection under the king of Moab. Finally, after receiving a word from God he moves into the forest of Hereth.

David is fleeing for his life. I want you to imagine what you would be feeling if the most powerful person in the land has promised to kill you once he finds you. I know I would be overcome with fear and probably anger as well. I would ask God, what did I do to deserve this? Why aren't you helping me?

David is altogether a different sort of person. He is convinced that God is on his side. That divine trust has transformed him into the kind of leader Israel has been waiting for. Even while David is fleeing for his life, hundreds of men begin to follow him. The Bible describes these followers as "All those who were in distress or in debt or discontented gathered around him, and he became their commander." The Hebrew words give us an even deeper look into the condition of these men. They were bitter. They wanted revenge. They wanted justice for the wrongs they had experienced under King Saul.

Usually these kinds of emotions lead to riots and needless violence, but none of this happened under the leadership of David. David had every right to be angry, bitter and fearful but instead he chose to place all of these concerns into the hands of God. I want you to read again the line David speaks in verse 3: "until I learn what God will do for me."

How many of us think this way – that God will do for us? David was able to push aside his negative emotions because he knew the character of God. He knew all of his trouble, all of his running, would not be in vain because God was up to something. And the men who were following David saw this too.

Deep, authentic trust in God does two things. First, it purifies the spirit. Second, it transforms those who are near it. David was changed by his trust in God and everyone who was near him experienced a transformation of their own as well.

44

God was on David's side because David did not have a side of his own. Everything he was and hoped to become depended on God showing up.

Takeaway: Trust in God transforms us.

Prayer: Forgive me God for not always trusting you like I should. Help me to depend on you and to remember that you have my best in mind.

When Fear Leads

Day 12
1 Samuel 22:6-23

The fall of Saul continues in this story as he makes his way to Nob, retracing the path taken by David. Saul begins by convincing his men that they have nothing to gain by David becoming king. Like any dictator, Saul was reminding his people the best life they could have is the one they have right now, under his leadership.

One of Saul's men, Doeg, steps forward and reveals how the priests helped David by giving him food and a weapon. This infuriates Saul and he condemns all of the priests to death.

Saul gives the order to slaughter them but his own guards refuse to budge. They know Saul has begun to lose it, but this is certainly going too far. Killing priests was equivalent to attacking God and no one wanted to be on Saul's side when God decided to attack back.

Once again, Doeg steps forward and enacts Saul's order. Eighty-five priests died that day. However, Saul was still not satisfied so he ordered his group to kill every living thing in the town. Only one man, a priest, escaped and fled into David's protection.

Over and over again, the story of Saul causes us to ask how can one man fall so far from God? Saul, the first king of Israel chosen by God himself, is now one of the most dangerous men in the land.

Saul stands in stark contrast to the story of David we saw in the previous verses. Just as trust can transform a person, so can fear. Saul was scared of many things. He was fearful of losing his power, his life, and his control.

When we are controlled by fear, it disables us from using logic or patience. The emotion causes us to move at twice the speed but without any direction. Living a life controlled by fear is like lighting a firecracker inside a glassware shop – no matter which way it goes, things are bound to get broken.

Takeaway: Trusting ourselves always leads to fearful living.

Prayer: God, I do not want to live a life characterized by fear. Take my trust off of myself and place it on to you.

Against God's Will

Day 13
1 Samuel 23:1-13

David is continuing to escape and hide from Saul when he receives word that one of the Israelite towns has been attacked by Philistine raiders. Despite fearing for his own safety, David still wants to protect the people of his country. He prays and God tells him to go protect his people.

After David's victory, Saul finds out about his location and immediately sends his own army to attack. However, David is once again ahead of the curve and receives a word from God that tells him to keep moving. David and his men quickly gather their things and head back out into the wilderness to fight another day.

There is a small but important element in this story that will get missed if you read it too quickly. If you remember from yesterday's text, Saul killed all the priests of Nob except for one. This man, who was also a priest, managed to escape and come under the protection of David. That priest was named Abiathar.

Abiathar is the one God spoke through to tell David about the Philistines and later, about Saul's army. A commentator writes the following about this scene, "for all of Saul's dogged pursuit, David, with a priest of Yahweh at his side, will never come to harm."[viii] Saul is fighting a battle he cannot win because he is trying to go against God's will. David is fighting a battle he cannot lose because he is on the side of God's plan.

That right there is the essence of the Christian life. When we attempt to go against God's will for our lives, it feels like we are swimming upstream. Maybe there will be some smooth portions of the journey, but the destination will leave us dissatisfied and disheartened.

Going in the direction of God's plan is not always easy either. But the benefit of choosing this route is that God will be right there with you every step of the way. Being a Christian should give us an unfair advantage in this life. I don't know what that looks like for you but I believe the story of David tells us we should have higher expectations of God's action in our lives.

David lived in such a way that he needed God to show up constantly. What would our stories look like if we followed his example?

Takeaway: When we don't expect much from God, it's because our trust in him is small.

Prayer: Father, it is hard for me to trust. Help me see your hand in my life today so that I can learn to expect great things from you.

Saul Spared Part 1

Day 14
1 Samuel 24:1-22

There are no coincidences when God is writing the story. Saul had gathered a new army of men and set out to find David. On his way, he stops to use the bathroom in one of the caves alongside the road. Of all caves in that area, he ends up using the very one David and his men were hiding in. Finally, David has his chance to end this conflict once and for all.

David's men urge him on to kill Saul, saying that this moment was promised by God (a promise the readers have not seen). Quietly, David sneaks up and cuts off a piece of Saul's robe to show him how close he truly was; but he restrains from hurting his king.

After Saul has finished and walks down to his men, David calls out and shows him the piece of robe he cut off. Saul is flooded with emotions: fear, guilt, anger, disappointment. He repeats the words of his son Jonathan, David will one day be king. Saul then returns home defeated.

This is one of the most incredible stories in David's saga. The sole reason for David's pain was here, sitting unguarded and completely vulnerable. And yet, David chose to keep his hand from violence and allow God to avenge the wrongs that have been done to him.

All of us have been wronged at some point in our lives, some far more so than others. Some of us try to ignore the pain. Others explain it away. A small percentage actually go and seek revenge. But the smallest group are the ones who learn to forgive.

David had every right to take revenge against Saul. The man had destroyed his life, killed hundreds of innocent people, and polluted the position God had placed him in. But two things kept David's anger at bay. First, God's choice of making Saul king. Second, God's choice of making David king.

David knew in his heart that both his own life and Saul's life were in the hands of God. He respected God enough not take vengeance for himself, but to let God be God in this situation. What would happen would go down in God's timing.

Takeaway: When we choose not to forgive, we are choosing to trust our own judgment over God's.

Prayer: Lord, everything comes back to trusting you. Build in me the capacity to forgive and the restraint to let you be God in my life.

Beyond Us

Day 15
1 Samuel 25:1

There is no explanation given. No preface, no warning. Just like that, Samuel, the last judge of Israel and one of the greatest prophets of their history, is gone.

The Bible says all of Israel mourned for him. Perhaps Saul even let David attend the funeral peacefully. We simply do not know because we are given so little about an event that must have meant so much.

Samuel was David's guide in many ways. He was the one who awoke the call in him to be king. Samuel was also the one who helped David time and time again throughout his life. If David didn't feel alone before, he certainly did now.

But maybe the brevity of Samuel's death shows us something about the way he thought about life. The stories of the Bible are constantly trying to get their characters to look beyond themselves. Abraham's life was a seed that would sprout countless descendants. Job's experience with pain would echo throughout time as a reminder of God's justice.

Samuel knew his life only meant something because of God. God had chosen to bring him into the service of the temple and eventually, make Samuel the kingmaker of Israel. Samuel's life mattered so much because he chose to play a small role in a very big story.

We have that same opportunity. When we reach our final day and celebrate what we have accomplished, instead of looking at how full we made our life we should seek to understand how we helped further the story. The story of God's work upon the earth. The story of broken humans being made whole again. The story of the ultimate Lover and the bride He would not give up on.

Our stories matter most when we focus on making ourselves matter least. Samuel's legacy led to one of the greatest dynasties of Israel's history, and eventually, to the king of kings himself. Never underestimate the role God has asked you to play.

Takeaway: Our lives matter most when they are part of something bigger than ourselves.

Prayer: Lord, please use me for Your good works. I want my life to count for something big.

The Frustrating Tools of God

Day 16
1 Samuel 25:2-44

After Samuel's death, the rest of the chapter tells the story of David and his conflict with a man named Nabal.

Nabal was a nasty sort of man. He was mean to his own family, his workers, and strangers alike. It was customary at this time that wealthy individuals gave a sort of thank you payment to those who kept their flocks safe.[ix] Usually, armed men would come and steal from the shepherds unless there were other armed men nearby (like David's group). However, when David sought this out from Nabal he refused, and this sent our typically calm leader into an anger-driven march.

David and his men quickly gathered their weapons and headed to take over all that Nabal had. Before they could follow through with their plan, Nabal's wife Abigail intervened. She calmed David down and quietly brought them what they were owed.

Shortly after, Nabal found out what happened, had a heart attack, and died ten days later. The story ends with David marrying the woman who helped him and kept him from unneeded bloodshed.

The simplest lessons are often the ones we forget. They become cliché, and we discount their wisdom. Not because they are wrong, but because we have become too familiar with them.

The two lessons David forgot in this scene were the following. First, God always works through people, so you never know what good thing a stranger could bring into your life. Second, we should always leave vengeance up to God. Without Abigail's intervention, David would have had a Saul moment.

There will always be those people who do not play fair in our lives. Maybe you interacted with one of them today. People who puts themselves first and couldn't care less about any other person. Remember this, God can still work through these people.

Through Nabal, God brought Abigail and David together. After Nabal's death, David married the widowed wife. This was another important piece of the puzzle for making David king.

Never discount an interaction. Never let a conflict make you forget who is truly in control. God is up to something, even in the most frustrating of moments.

Takeaway: God uses every kind of person to accomplish His plans.

Prayer: Father, help me be patient in every situation. My story is in your hands and no person can disrupt what you are doing.

Saul Spared Part 2

Day 17
1 Samuel 26:1-25

For a second time, Saul's life is spared by the very person he has been trying to destroy.

As David continues to flee and hide out in various places, the people of Ziph see him and notify Saul. Saul takes advantage of the new information and leaves at once with his army by his side. If we fast-forward a short while we see Saul and his men asleep in their camp only a short distance away from David and his men.

David decides to sneak into the camp and show Saul, once again, that he means him no harm. David is able to get all the way up to where Saul is sleeping. Quickly, David takes his spear and water jug and runs out of the camp.

Once he has run a safe distance, David turns back and calls to the men of the camp so that he can show how close he was to killing the king once again. Saul and his men are dumbfounded, just as they were before, and both parties go their separate ways.

How do we know when the options before us are from God or are simply a temptation? David had the opportunity to end his problems once and for all because God put his enemies in a deep sleep (*verse 12*). But he chose not to out of respect for Saul's position in relation to God.

We will probably never have such a clear opportunity in our lives as David did. But what we will have are moments when we have to decide between two options: am I in control of my story or am I allowing God to guide my life?

Controlling our story almost never looks wrong. In fact, it makes perfect sense. We make the logical choices, take the path that is clearly in front of us, and thank God when things work out. God's version of our story is not the same as ours. David trusted God and took the less logical path. He took the option that included risk and danger and required him to put his life and wellbeing completely in the hands of God.

No one can tell you what choices you should make. What I can do, and what Scripture does, is show you that trusting God is always the better option even when it doesn't make sense upfront.

Takeaway: God's illogical path is better than our logical one.

Prayer: Almighty God, thank you that you do not have to play inside the rules and that you create amazing stories with ordinary people. Help me have faith in the path you choose for me.

Trust Fails

Day 18
1 Samuel 27:1-12

Whether out of fear or wisdom, David decides to leave his homeland and take refuge in the land of his enemies, the Philistines.

David and his men deceptively pledge their allegiance to Achish, king of Gath. He gives them a small town named Ziklag in exchange for their military service. David and his men accept and make the town their home base of operations. However, they do not attack their homeland as promised. Instead, they raid and destroy other nearby towns which belong to the allies of the Philistines, always careful to make sure no evidence was left behind.

The king buys it and, for a time, David is safe from every one of his enemies.

This is a difficult scene to understand within the bigger story of David's rise to power. Every step of the way, it seems as though David was willing to sacrifice whatever it took to trust God and do things His way. But now here he was, living in a foreign land and making friends with a foreign king.

Our commentator, Dr. McCarter Jr., says the following about this chapter: "[this story] functions in the larger narrative as a further example of David's ingenuity and ability to succeed in the most hostile circumstances."[x] This scene focuses on what David is capable of when he is a man apart from God.

I believe this story is both a warning and a foreshadow. It warns us that no one will be able to trust God fully one hundred percent of the time. We are human, just as the chosen king of Israel was human, and mistakes will happen. This scene foreshadows an element of David which we have hardly seen so far – his similarity to Saul. Just like Saul, David is able to get people to like him, trust him, and follow him. And just like Saul, David will become his own greatest enemy at times.

We will all fail to trust God at one point or another in our lives but we can have hope because God does not give up so easily on us.

Takeaway: Even the best of us will fail to trust God, but He is patient.

Prayer: Father, you are more wise than I can imagine and more patient than I deserve. Help me trust you, and when I don't, quickly bring me back to where I need to be.

Ignoring God

Day 19
1 Samuel 28:3-25

As Saul nears the end of his reign as king, we see him take stranger and more desperate actions in order to keep his claim to power.

War was on the horizon. The Philistines gathered on the borders of Israel, and Saul gathered his forces as well. However, this would be the first time Saul was truly alone in battle. He had always had God, Samuel or David on his side. Now he had no one.

In a desperate plea for guidance he seeks a ghostwife also called a medium.[xi] These individuals could speak with the dead, or at the very least, could speak to something not of this world. The ghostwife is fearful because her practice has been outlawed and now, here was the very king who outlawed it asking her to perform for him. Reluctantly, the woman calls up Samuel's spirit and he appears before Saul.

Saul gets the opposite of what he had hoped. Instead of guidance and encouragement, Samuel tells him he will die in battle and the kingdom will go to David. Saul falls to the ground, struck by fear.

This episode was provoked by God's silence towards Saul in verse 6. Saul's story will soon come to an end and there is nothing he can do to change that. Yet, if God had spoken to Saul, maybe this scene would have never happened. Maybe Saul's life could have come to a less violent end. Why did God choose to be silent?

The simple answer is disobedience. Saul repeatedly chose to go his own way over God's way. More than that, he stopped even considering God's guidance as an option until he was in the most desperate of situations. Commentator Robert Chisholm Jr. writes "communication is a two-way street."[xii] It's not that God chose to stop speaking, but Saul tuned out God's voice. And when he tried to tune God back in, He had nothing more to say.

It's hard to read stories like this about God. While He is all-loving, slow to anger and quick to forgive, He does choose to be in a relationship with us. If, like Saul, we choose to ignore Him except for when we want something – what kind of response do you think we will get?

Communication with God goes both ways. Pray and listen. Open yourself up to Him by saying what is on your heart, but also by responding to what He has asked you to do. Otherwise, you will find that your one-sided relationship with God is actually no relationship at all.

Takeaway: Healthy communication with God goes both ways.

Prayer: Thank you Lord that You want a real relationship with me. Please help me to hear what You are asking me to do and to know that You hear me too.

For The Undeserving

Day 20
1 Samuel 30:23-25

During Saul's encounter with the witch of Endor, a lot has been happening for David and his men. The king of the Philistines called to meet with them and told David and his men that they would not be going to battle against the Israelites. The other Philistine leaders were afraid that David might switch sides mid-battle, a very wise fear for them to have.

While David and his men were gone from their base in Ziklag, a group of Amalekite raiders came and stole away all of their families and goods. Immediately, David assembled two-thirds of his men to recapture what was taken from them. Before long, they found the enemy's camp and won back everything that had been stolen.

The strange part of this story occurs when David's army returns home to the one-third of the men who remained. The ones who fought wanted to keep the goods for themselves, and only return the families of those who stayed behind. David was not going to let this happen.

He stood up and said, "*The share of the man who stayed with the supplies is to be the same as that of him who went down to the battle. All will share alike.*" From then on, this idea was a rule throughout Israel.

Reaching forward, we see Jesus present this same idea in the New Testament: "*I sent you to reap what you have not worked for. Others have done the hard work, and you have reaped the benefits of their labor.*" (John 4:38)

So what does this mean for us? This is another unfair advantage of trusting God. We live in a culture that has made effort, ambition and striving the most important qualities. There is nothing wrong with any of those. But God knows when we focus on those attributes alone we miss out on dependence, patience and the understanding of what it means to receive grace.

God gives unfairly to the undeserving. That is why we have the amazing gift of salvation! That is also why we should place our life concerns into the hands of God. He doesn't play by the rules; He doesn't have to. And we benefit by belonging to Him.

Takeaway: God can and does solve our problems by giving us what we do not deserve.

Prayer: Father, help me to believe that my good life does not entirely depend upon me. Show me that you are my unfair advantage.

Saul's Incomplete Story

Day 21
1 Samuel 31:1-13

The first book of Samuel ends on the tragic note of Saul's demise.

The Philistines and Israelites have finally met in battle. Both sides are pushing and taking heavy losses. This scene reminds us how far Israel has come since we saw David stepping out to fight Goliath. However, this battle will have a much different outcome.

Before long, the Philistines have the advantage and Saul and his men are surrounded. Saul calls to his armor-bearer to slay him, at least then he will die with some honor. But the armor-bearer is afraid and refuses. Out of a mix of courage and fear, Saul falls upon his own sword, ending the life of the first king of Israel.

The Philistines take the bodies of Saul and his men and display them to show their victory, but that night a group of people from Jabesh Gilead steal the bodies back and give them an honorable burial.

One word comes to mind when you read this passage: incomplete.[xiii] We are left with so many questions. Did Saul repent to God before his death? What will happen to the rest of his family? Does this make David the official king? Many of these questions will be answered in the chapters to come, but the idea of incompleteness offers us a unique insight into the character of Saul.

Saul lived as an incomplete person. There were always more enemies to defeat, more alliances to be made, and more pleasure to be experienced. Saul defined himself more by what he did not have, than by what he did.

A life lived apart from God will always feel incomplete. It's cliché to say that God fills up the hole that is in our hearts, but this idea is terrifyingly true as we see in the life of Saul. There is something inside of us that hungers for more and it can only be satisfied in two ways. First, by always chasing the more (money, pleasure, prestige), even to the detriment of everything else in our lives. Second, by chasing the One who is more than enough.

Takeaway: Whenever our eyes are on anything other than God, our lives will appear incomplete.

Prayer: Dear God, please help me to not live a life that feels incomplete. I know you are good, but help me believe it through the things I decide to pursue.

Promises Through Pain

Day 22
2 Samuel 1:1-15

In the aftermath of Saul's death, a deceptive messenger comes into David's presence.

David had gone off to fight the Amalekites while the Israelites and Philistines did battle. Once David returned to his temporary home, a young man brought him the news that Saul was finally dead and that he is now king. More than that, the messenger tells David that he was the one to kill Saul since he found him defeated and wishing for death.

Most commentators agree that this man was making up a story in order to gain favor from David.[xiv] However, the man's story has the opposite effect. David tears off his clothes in mourning and goes on to lament the deaths of Saul and his family. He also takes the messenger and puts him to death. No matter how terrible Saul was, David believed no one should hurt God's anointed.

The second book of Samuel begins on a note of grief. David never wanted to come into his kingship like this. But as we will see, this is by no means the end of David's troubles.

What is keeping you from the position God has called you to? Perhaps it is a position of authority, a position of freedom, or a position of renewal.

David had to deal with Saul in order to fulfill the call God had put on his life. However, David did not "deal" with Saul according to human wisdom. He didn't bad-mouth him, he never showed the king disrespect, and he refused to lay a hand on the man even when Saul had promised to kill him.

David rested in God's promise, knowing that God would fulfill it in His timing and according to His way.

God will bring you to what He has promised, but always within His timeframe and according to His way. We may have to come into our position through grief and pain and patience, but we will get there. The kingship was always David's, but it had to come through Saul's sorrow.

Takeaway: God will always fulfill His promise to us.

Prayer: Lord, thank You that You are always faithful and always good. Help me to focus not on the current situation but on the promise You have placed on my life.

In God's Timing

Day 23
2 Samuel 2:1-4

As we move into the beginning of David's reign as king we see a glimmer of his inner-most character.

The stage is set for David's rise. Saul is dead, the competing nations, like the Philistines, have just exhausted themselves from war, and David has everything he needs in order to become the next king of Israel.

Instead of marching in and taking what is rightfully his, David does the one thing that has continually set him apart: rely fully on God. Before he does anything, David asks God two questions: *What should I do? And where should I go?*

The Lord answers him by telling him to go to a place called Hebron. There are many ideas as to why God told David to go to that specific place. Perhaps it had to do with politics or geography. However, I believe the most convincing reason is that the city of Hebron was historically important. It was connected to the lineage of the patriarchs, like Abraham.[xv] God told David to go there because He wanted everyone to know that He was continuing to fulfill the promises He made all those centuries before.

Once David arrived, the people of that region crowned David King of Judah. He had finally succeeded.

I cannot stress enough the importance of how David came into his rule. Time and time again, David has opportunities in his story to "skip ahead" and take what has been promised to him. But time and time again he chooses to wait on God.

Don't forget who is writing your story. When we are lost, confused, and frustrated it's easier to trust God for amazing things to happen because we are unable to see the next steps that we need to take. It can be much more difficult when things are good, because that is when we think we can take back control of our story.

Whether you are on a mountaintop, or steeped in a valley, wait on God's direction. He will always take you further than you could have gone on your own.

Takeaway: Trust God as much in good times as you do in bad times.

Prayer: Lord, you know why I am here and how best to help me fulfill my purpose. Give me patience to look to you instead of trying to control my own story.

What The Reward Requires

Day 24
2 Samuel 3:1

The first verse of chapter 3 provides a useful summary for the unfolding situation.

While David has been crowned king, his rule is incomplete. He has control over the region of Judah while Saul's son, Ishb-Bosheth, has been crowned king over Israel (think of it as the north versus the south).

The two royal houses quickly begin to attack one another. Small skirmishes turned into sanctioned representative combat. This is when a few fighters from each side are chosen to represent the whole army.[xvi] Before long, these battles escalated into full-fledged warfare and the nation of Israel found itself immersed in a civil war.

There is not much hope in these chapters, aside from the fact that David appears to be winning. Slowly but surely, his side is gaining the upper hand.

A friend of mine recently bought his first house. It's a beautiful starter home with a modern layout and lots of space. However, I was surprised when my friend told me how different owning a home was from his expectations. He went on to list all the things that constantly needed fixing, and all the things he didn't even think about before he owned his house (like dealing with a pesky groundhog).

Like David, my friend got what he wanted but when it finally came it was much different than he expected.

Attaining the promise God has given you is not the end of the journey. The ending of one story is always the beginning of another. David had to fight his way into the kingship, and once he finally had the crown, he had to keep fighting!

How is this supposed to be encouraging? Christians often believe that you need endurance to reach the reward, which is true. But it doesn't end there. The reward continues to require endurance. The lessons God teaches us along the way are not meant to be forgotten at the finish line. Instead, they are the foundation of what God wants to continue to build in us.

Takeaway: Every crown we achieve is both the end and beginning of our growth.

Prayer: Father, thank you for how far you have brought me. Now that I am here, give me the endurance to keep going.

The Ends and the Means

Day 25
2 Samuel 4:1-12; 5:3

David's struggle in his new authority continues and reaches a new level as dangerous events unfold in Israel.

The king of Israel, Ish-Bosheth is beginning to falter and those loyal to David take advantage of the situation. During one evening, they sneak into the king's home while he is asleep and take his life. With evidence in hand, they run off to show David that they have helped his cause.

However, if you remember what happened just a few chapters before with the death of Saul, then you will know what lies ahead for these devious men. They proudly tell David about their exploit but before they can even finish, David gives the order to have them killed. He will not allow evil men to do his bidding.

Still, the death of Ish-Bosheth was the key. A few verses later in chapter 5, David is crowned king of Israel – once again uniting the entire territory under one rule and fulfilling the whole promise of God.

This scene presents us with a very difficult theological concept. I will try and choose my words very carefully, but there is no real way to soften the idea. At times, God will use the evil deeds of the lost to benefit the story He is writing for His chosen.

Perhaps Ish-Bosheth would have died from an illness or another enemy of Israel could have taken his life. But that is not what happened. People loyal to David, men who believed in God and His work took it upon themselves to commit an evil deed and "fast-forward" David's rule.

David benefited from the sin of his men.

What lesson could this story have for us? Is it true that our stories may benefit from the sin of others: yes. Is it right for evil means to be used to accomplish good ends: no.

None of us will make it out of this life unscathed and unpolluted by evil. What we can do is not let one evil deed justify another. David quickly put those two men to rest because he wanted to send a message. His message was that evil deeds are not rewarded in his kingdom.

You may be promoted because of someone else's failure, or even given a life-saving organ because another human made a bad decision. Always repay evil with good and remember who is ultimately in control of our stories.

Takeaway: Evil has its role to play in this world, but God is still supreme.

Prayer: Almighty God, I wish evil did not exist. I see how it corrupts and confuses and I know how easily I can fall into it. Please give me enough wisdom and strength for this day.

He Is Not Safe

Day 26
2 Samuel 6:1-15

After David's succession into kingship he took it upon himself to bring the ark of God into his capital city.

During this move, the ark began to tip and one of the men reached out to make sure it did not hit the ground. As soon as the man's hand touched the ark he was struck dead. The atmosphere of celebration quickly turned into one of fear. David decided to reroute the ark to a foreigner's land. There it would stay until David changed his mind.

Thankfully, it did not take long. David saw how much the foreigner was being blessed and so he made a second attempt to bring it into his city. This time it was even more of a fanfare with sacrifices, music and dancing. The ark arrived safely into the City of David, with the king dancing for all to see.

There is an uncomfortable dichotomy every Christian must face when getting to know what

God is really like. On the one hand, He is our good Father who wants to take care of us and bless us. And on the other hand, He is the supreme ruler over all creation who is slow to anger but uncompromising in His standards.

In this short passage we see both elements of God's character placed side by side. David was terrified after the incident with the ark. It took seeing another person's blessing to remind him how good God really is.

If we spend any length of time growing as a Christian, we are going to run into these moments. Moments where the reality of God scares us to our core. Where we learn something about our Heavenly Father which catches us off guard or makes us weary of learning more about Him.

Let me tell you, it's okay. This is part of the Christian journey. Learning to fear God is the surest way to build your trust in Him. It is difficult, but it is necessary.

In C.S. Lewis' book *The Lion, the Witch, and the Wardobe*, Susan finally sees that the person they have been looking for is not actually a person at all. Instead, Aslan is a lion. She is frightened by this and asks her guide, *is he safe?* The character answers, *Course he isn't safe. But he's good. He's the King.*

Takeaway: Fearing God is part of building our trust in Him.

Prayer: God, help me to know the real you – the encouraging and the intimidating. And help me trust you through the process.

A Godward Story

Day 27
2 Samuel 7:1-17

After the revelation of God's complex character, we get one of the longest speeches from God in the Old Testament. David, now relatively settled after all the trials that catapulted him into kingship, sees that Israel has the opportunity and resources to build a great temple for God.

Yet the time is not right. God answers David through the prophet Nathan – a fancy temple is not His priority. God is doing something infinitely larger than what David can understand. This kingdom and David's kingship are only the very tip of an iceberg that will stretch across countless generations and set up the True King who will reign without end.

God goes on to bless David and declare that Israel will come into a season of prosperity. It is a powerful statement and an almost unbelievable promise. David has everything he could already want and now, here is God promising him that more good things are on their way.

The thing about the Bible that makes you want to keep reading and digging is that it never goes the way you think it will. Every story has twists and turns you would never expect. Each chapter is a new experience and a new perspective on what God is really like.

God wants us to be interested in the story He is writing. He invites us in by doing incredible works and then turning to us and asking, would you like to be a part of what I am doing?

David said yes. That willingness began his ascent to the throne and his trust in God helped him succeed where Saul had failed.

We have to ask ourselves are we more concerned with writing our own stories than we are with becoming a part of God's? If we pay attention to the story of David what we see is a man obsessed with wanting to do things God's way. As the Scriptures reveal, God's way leads to an unexplainable life.

A shepherd boy made king. These are the kinds of stories God writes. This is the kind of story God is inviting you to be a part of.

Takeaway: Truly great lives are directed by God.

Prayer: Thank you Father that you write incredible stories. Please take my life and make it great, make it count, make it yours.

The Three Ingredients For A Miracle

Day 28
2 Samuel 9:1-12

David continues to gain victory after victory and expand his new kingdom into a truly sizable force. Yet, he still takes time to remember the promises he made and honor those who have helped him along the way.

By now it has been years since the death of his close friend, Jonathan, the son of Saul. But time has not dampened his love for him. In this chapter David starts a search for any remaining descendants of Saul so that he can show them kindness for the sake of his friend. His servants eventually find a lame man (meaning he couldn't walk) named Mephibosheth.

It was customary for the ruling house to completely wipe away any descendants from the previous power. That way they could ensure any greedy or angry family members would not try to overthrow the kingdom. David could have done that with Mephibosheth. He was handicapped, poor and saw himself as having no value. But David chose a different path and Mephibosheth bravely answered his call.

David chose to honor the man as an overflow of his love for Jonathan. Mephibosheth instantly became one of the richest men in the kingdom and had a place at the king's table for every meal.

This scene becomes even more meaningful when you realize what Mephibosheth's name means. It's a difficult combination of words, but put simply it means the *dispeller of shame*.[xvii] God chose this lame, poor man to bring an end to one of the most furious feuds in Biblical history. Because of God's grace, David's kindness, and Mephibosheth's bravery – the house of David and the house of Saul were finally at peace.

This three-part structure is often all it takes for miracles to happen in our own lives. First, the Bible makes it clear that God's grace is consistently shown towards us. Second, because of that grace we should learn to expect uncommon kindness – not only from those who know us but also from our sworn enemies. Can you guess what the third part is?

Our bravery.

Mephibosheth was able to be brave because he believed God was good. He believed that his name was not a mistake. That even though most of his life had been characterized by shame and loss, it was not going to be how his story ended. And as we can see, that one act of bravery and trust launched him into an entirely new life.

Perhaps many of the prayers we think God has not answered are actually just waiting for us to bravely step towards them. We serve the same God as Mephibosheth and His plans are no less good.

Takeaway: God's grace, human kindness, and personal bravery make the impossible happen.

Prayer: Dear Lord, help me to be brave in the difficult parts of my life. I know you are good, so help me trust that goodness by taking action.

The Third Sin

Day 29
2 Samuel 11:1-16, 26-27

As we enter the second half of Samuel's second book, a much different picture of David begins to arise. Up to this point the text has mainly focused upon his accomplishments. David has been a model citizen and a shining contrast to Saul. David was the hope of Israel. Sure, he made a few mistakes along the way but all in all he was God's chosen king and acted like it.

Now we enter into a season of trouble. Why David's story takes the dark turn that it does will be explored as we continue. Here, we must focus on the chapter at hand and on David's two great sins.

While his army was away, David remained in his palace. One night he happened to see a beautiful woman named Bathsheba bathing. Without considering the consequences of his actions, he had the married woman brought to him and slept with her.

It wasn't long until he found out she had become pregnant. Fearful of losing his honor, David tries to cover up the situation by having her husband, Uriah, come home from war and sleep with her. Yet David's plan fails because Uriah wants to uphold his commitment to the army and not enjoy his home and wife while his fellow Israelites are still off at war. Out of options, David has Uriah placed in the frontlines so that he is killed in the next battle. David and Bathsheba's honor is safe, at least for the time being. The chapter ends with David officially marrying her and we are left with a foreboding statement, "But the thing David had done displeased the Lord."

This chapter is usually called the two great sins because David commits both adultery and murder in a short amount of time. But if you read the first verse carefully, there is a third sin David commits.

The first line reads, "at the time when kings go off to war." The writer is setting the expectation that we are going to read about David winning more battles for Israel. Instead, we read that David has sent out his commander Joab in his place and chose to remain in Jerusalem.

You see, David's first sin was pride. He elected to not fulfill his duties as king and began to fall down a very dangerous path.

We wonder how could someone as good as David fall so far so quickly? The answer is almost always that the person let a seed of pride take root. David had plenty of opportunities to murder the man who was trying to kill him, but refused. In past stories, David has always been a model of respect towards woman. But now, as king, he allowed the same sin that consumed Saul to take up root in him.

This story is a warning to all of us. When we turn from trusting God to trusting ourselves we are beginning down a slippery slope. David never intended to cause so much pain, but when we act apart from God that is all we can do. As we will see, nothing goes unnoticed by God.

Takeaway: The simple sin of pride can lead us down a path we never imagined.

Prayer: Holy God, forgive me for my pride. Protect me from thinking that I know better than You – I know You only want good for me.

Relentless Forgiveness

Day 30
2 Samuel 12:1-14, 24-25

Not long after David commits the pair of atrocities, the prophet Nathan enters the scene. As one could guess, Nathan knows what has happened and has come on God's behalf to call David out.

There are no introductions, no welcomes. As soon as Nathan spots David he dives into the parable of the rich and poor men. David hears the story and it infuriates him. He will not allow such an injustice in his kingdom. That is when Nathan fires back, "You are the man!"

Convicted, broken, fearful – David admits his sin and pleads for forgiveness. Nathan, again speaking for God, forgives David on the spot. But this does not excuse him from the consequences of his actions. The child David and Bathsheba had together will die as punishment.

On some level we know God will always find out our sin. Yet still, we try to hide. We lie about it and cover it up, thinking that with enough time everything will just blow over.

I want to be very clear, as clear as Scripture is itself: God will not forget. He is a just God and a good Father and He will not hold back from disciplining His children when they fail.

At the same time, it's impossible to read these verses and not see the grace strewn throughout. The first thing Nathan says to David after David admits his sin is that God has forgiven him. God hates sin because it separates us from being in relationship with him. He punishes us not to push us further away, but to encourage us to cling to Him. The second act of grace is that David and Bathsheba have another child together who will end up being David's rightful heir: Solomon.

God never wants painful sin to be a part of our story. But it's also clear that sin never has to be the end of our story with God. Forgiveness is always available. Your family may not give it to you. The people you hurt may not give it to you. But God always will.

Takeaway: No matter our sin, God is standing by to forgive us and bring us back to Him.

Prayer: Father, thank You for being willing to take away my sin and make me new again. Keep me near to You and help me make the most of Your forgiveness.

The Problem With Silencing Pain

Day 31
2 Samuel 13:1-22

There are few scenes as brutal and sordid as the one we find in this chapter. One of David's sons, Amnon, has begun to lust after one of David's daughters, Tamar.

A union, or marriage, between the two would have been acceptable. They were half siblings and marrying within one's extended family was an accepted practice. But Amnon was not interested in doing things the right way.

One evening, he conned his way into being alone with Tamar and took advantage of her. Afterward, to add insult to injury, he forced her back out into the streets.

Tamar's brother, Absalom, found her and asked what happened. He could see the answer across his sister's face. But rather than taking the issue up with their father, King David, they kept the matter silent.

Did you ever get the chance to work with petri dishes in school? They are small glass circular containers used for growing bacteria. The way you use them is by introducing some small amount of bacteria into the dish, closing it up, and allowing the bacteria to grow. The petri dish blocks out almost all interferences, so the culture is able to grow. When your experiment is finished, the microscopic spot of bacteria now covers the entire inside of the petri dish.

Pain operates the same way. Tamar was hurt in one of the worst ways a person can be. Absalom wanted to protect her and did what he thought was best, which was to keep the incident quiet. But silence can be the most damaging option.

When we keep pain silent inside ourselves, it's like introducing bacteria to a petri dish. At first, it's hardly visible. We know it's there, but if we try hard enough we can ignore it. Overtime that becomes harder and harder to do. The small pain grows in silence. It begins to expand within you and ignoring it eventually becomes impossible.

When the pain feels like it has grown bigger than us, that is when we make dangerous choices. As we will see, Absalom's well-meaning gesture to his sister eventually erupted into something far beyond what anyone could have guessed.

Takeaway: Pain that is kept silent will eventually grow out of our control.

Prayer: Lord, help me not to run from my pain but to face it with your strength.

Defining Ourselves

Day 32
2 Samuel 13:28-29; 15:1-12

Absalom's anger and pain continued to fester until there was no more room to contain it.

First, Absalom took revenge against his brother Amnon, the one who had hurt his sister. However, the king's children were rarely alone so when it says that Absalom killed his brother it's likely that it included the murder of dozens of bodyguards, servants and friends.[xviii] Absalom's anger had erupted and killing all those people was just the beginning.

Next, Absalom turned his anger against his father. Perhaps he blamed him for not handling the situation correctly But didn't he choose to keep it quiet so David didn't know?. Or maybe, this was the only outlet he could think of. Regardless of the reason, Absalom began making moves to overthrow his father's kingdom.

Through clever campaigning Absalom "stole the hearts of the people of Israel." Slowly but surely, he began to amass a huge network of support.

Then, after a few years, Absalom traveled to Hebron and declared himself king.

Absalom's story, like Saul's, is another instance of something taking a character further than they ever thought they would go. Saul's self-sufficiency led him down a path that ended in his suicide. David's pride took Israel's golden king and turned him into an adulterer and murderer. Absalom's pain transformed him from a caring son and brother into a manipulative murderer and false king.

When we read the Bible we have to remember that these were real people with real problems. Yes, the stories can be somewhat fantastic because they are set in a kingdom with prophets and a very present God, but the characters are no less human than us. We all have the potential to be Absalom.

Each of us has a pain we have kept silent for too long, or an anger we have let fester, or a sense of pride that runs as deep as our bones. The good news is that we have a God who is just as present now as he was back then.

We don't have to be controlled by the negatives in our lives. We can choose to hear God's call before it is too late, to set down our pain or anger or pride and let God be God.

Takeaway: My pain/anger/pride does not have to define me. God is the one who defines who I truly am.

Prayer: Thank you Lord that You have given me a different option. Please give me the strength to choose it, and to choose You over myself.

Action And Trust

Day 33
2 Samuel 15:13-15, 31; 17:11-14

After years of reigning as king, David finds himself fleeing for his life once again. This time from the wrath of his own son.

Whether or not Absalom's rebellion was another part of David's punishment (because of Uriah and Bathsheba) is up for debate. What matters is that as soon as David heard about Absalom's group, he quickly gathered his closest people and headed for safety. While he was traveling, he sent a handful of people back to Jerusalem. His hope was that by having people loyal to him close to the false king, he could gather information while also frustrating the plans of his new enemy.

When we jump forward to chapter 17, we can see that David's plan worked. Absalom's advisors were divided and ultimately the false king took the wrong advice (as we will soon see).

Is this another example of David trusting himself over God? Did he learn anything from the painful lesson of his child's death?

I believe this is a powerful example of David resubmitting himself to God once again. In 15:25-26, David says this as he exits the city he has called home now for many years, "If I find favor in the Lord's eyes, he will bring me back...But if he says, 'I am not pleased with you,' then I am ready; let him do to me whatever seems good to him."

David's heart is in the right place, back to trusting God. But what about his actions – we see him running, fearful, and planting seeds of deception for the false king. Can a trusting heart line up with cautious actions? To answer this, we turn back to the commentator Anderson, "The author [of 2 Samuel] sees human actions in the wider framework of the divine will, and therefore it is not a question of either/or."[xix]

To put it simply: yes, you can trust God and still take action towards what you want. In fact, I believe this is something the Bible teaches close readers over and over again. We have fallen into the trap of thinking that trusting God means doing little to nothing where in fact the opposite it true. Trusting God usually requires us to do more!

David fled because he trusted God. He could have stayed and tried to fight off his son, but that would have been out of his own strength. David submitted himself and believed that if God still wanted him to be king, then both David's and God's actions would come together to accomplish that goal.

Doing what you think is best and trusting God are not contradictory as long as your heart is submitted to Him. David could act as he did because his worth and hope were not tied up in the result, but in who God was. David wanted God more than he wanted the kingship, and because of that, he was able to act in the best interest of both.

Takeaway: Trusting God and taking action are not opposing options. They can work together when we are humble.

Prayer: Heavenly Father, thank You that You have equipped me with a sound mind, a grateful heart, and an ambitious spirit. Please use my actions for Your good, and keep me trusting You every step of the way.

The Cost of Answered Prayer

Day 34
2 Samuel 18:1-17

Absalom's rebellion reaches its climax in chapter 18 as both his and David's armies meet for battle.

We can only imagine the feeling that must have weighed heavy on everyone's hearts that day. This was even more of a civil war than when Saul and David had experienced their conflicts. Household against household, father against son.

David's men convince him to stay behind from battle. Whether due to his advanced age or his deep desire to protect Absalom – either way, they felt he would be more help from afar.

The battle commenced and both sides took heavy losses. After a short while, in a strange turn of events, Absalom found himself caught in a tree (his hair had gotten stuck in some branches) and surrounded by David's men. Despite David's plea to protect his son, the men end Absalom's life and give him the burial of an "accursed man."[xx] Israel's bloodiest civil war to date was now over.

David wanted a number of conflicting things. He wanted to be king again. He wanted to submit to God's will. And he wanted Absalom to be his son again. In a perfect world, maybe all three of these could have aligned. David could have regained the throne, Absalom would have asked for forgiveness and become a loyal servant, and God would have smiled down on the whole situation.

Unfortunately, for now we live in the real world – not a perfect one. Because of this, answered prayers will sometimes require loss.

David prayed for his men and his cause to be victorious. However, he likely did this while trying to ignore what it would mean for Absalom.

I want to encourage you to pray bold prayers, to pursue God's will ferociously and to aim towards a life of true impact. But along the way, do not forget to count the cost. Bold prayers often require brave forfeits. In our pursuit of God we will be required to drop the excess baggage we have chosen to carry. A life of big impact will usually forego many of life's little pleasures.

Takeaway: An answered prayer will sometimes be accompanied by a loss.

Prayer: Help me God to pray good prayers, but please also help me see the cost of what I may be asking. You give, You take away, and You are good.

Beyond Rules

Day 35
2 Samuel 20:1-22

The end of Absalom's rebellion was not the end of David's troubles. This conflict brought to light a lot of unresolved feelings throughout the kingdom. People in the North (Israel) were jealous of the people in the South (Judah). Remnants of Saul's family still held grudges against David's kingship. The kingdom as a whole was reluctant to put David back on the throne.[xxi]

One man tried to take advantage of this uncertainty. A man named Sheba attempted to amass a second rebellion as the king was making his way back to Jerusalem. David was not going to let this man divide the kingdom once again so he sent Joab to deal with those who had betrayed him.

Once they finally caught up with Sheba, it turned out that his threats consisted of little more than hot air. Many of the men had deserted him and once he was cornered inside a city, the people inside turned on him and ended his life. Yet, as we will see, David's troubles were still not over.

The rebellions of Absalom and Sheba are placed right next to each other in Scripture, which invites us to compare the two scenarios. In both, a person whom David trusted gains support and announces a rebellion. However, David handles these two conflicts in completely opposite ways.

When Absalom begins his rebellion, David immediately flees the city. When Sheba attempts his rebellion, David reaches the city of Jerusalem and stays there. David acted in two contradictory ways and yet both were avenues of trusting God.

The Bible is a very human book. God used humans to write stories about Him and other humans, and He now has humans teaching His book around the world. Humans have the bad habit of trying to fit everything into a category: good – bad, expensive – cheap, black – white. But so often in Scripture, God purposely breaks those categories.

David handled the same situation in two different ways and both of them were good. Be wary of anyone telling you there is only one way for you to trust God in any situation. Every story is different. God is not trying to get you to stick to a staunch rulebook. He is trying to get your eyes on Him!

Takeaway: Our priority must be following God rather than following rules.

Prayer: You are a real and active God. Don't let me take the easy route of just trying to follow all the rules, but push me to truly seek you in every trouble and every joy.

The Ripples of Sin

Day 36
2 Samuel 21:1-14

As we near the end of David's story, we hear about a famine that has lasted 3 years. This famine could have been going on during the last two rebellions (a hungry nation could explain why so many people were willing to go against the king). Regardless of when it began, the famine was another problem stacked onto the shoulders of David. So he turned to seek God's guidance.

What we discover is that the famine is actually punishment for one of Saul's sins. In his fury, Saul broke a treaty with the people of Gibeon and killed many of them. Even though the famine was Saul's fault, David takes it upon himself to make things right with the Gibeonites.

David turns over a small group of the last descendants of Saul, so the Gibeonites can take their revenge. Soon after, the famine lifts and David is free from one more trouble.

It seems unfair that all of Israel should have to suffer because of Saul. But this episode reminds us of one of God's core attributes: justice.

Commentator Chisholm Jr. writes, "This episode is a reminder that God is just. He takes up the cause of the victims of injustice and will eventually punish those who perpetrate crimes against others. ...Sin has unforeseen and persistent consequences, including the collateral damage it inflicts on innocent parties."[xxii]

Saul never intended to harm his own people when he attacked the Gibeonites. He was fueled by rage and power and did not try to control himself. If he knew it would have cost the lives of many of his own people, maybe he would have acted differently.

This is the dangerous thing about sin. We never know how far the ripple effect of its destruction will go. All we see is the immediate reward or satisfaction, never the consequences. Saul did not see the famine. David did not see the rebellions. How much can we not see as well?

Sin is always more destructive than we think, and touches more people than we can imagine. Thankfully, we serve a God who is more forgiving than we think, and who can reach and heal the ripples of our mistakes.

Takeaway: Our sins can have bigger consequences than we know.

Prayer: Father, please forgive me of my sins and heal those who have been hurt by my bad choices.

Faithful For The Faithless

Day 37
2 Samuel 22:1-30

This chapter offers us an intimate look into David's character once again. Amidst strife, famine and war David chooses to praise all that God has done for him.

In verse 1, David begins by saying "The Lord is my rock, my fortress and my deliverer" and goes on to proclaim how God has continually saved him from the people who have wanted to destroy his kingdom.

These verses, which are an echo of Psalm 18, reveal David's covenantal mentality. God has made a promise to David, that He will establish His kingdom and help him succeed – but on the condition that he remains faithful and obedient. David echoes this in the heart of his praise: "The Lord has dealt with me according to my righteousness...to the faithful you show yourself faithful."

The covenant idea says that as long as you do your part, I will do mine. What David saw and believed about God was not untrue, but it was incomplete.

In the Old Testament, God was revealing pieces of himself. Like an onion, peeling away the inner most truth. For Abraham, Jacob, David – He brought them into His fold through covenant promises. As the Old Testament continued, and God's relationship with Israel deepened, He began to reveal His truest nature.

God loves to go beyond expectations. By sending us Jesus, God showed that this was not a 50-50 relationship. Instead, it was 100% Him coming to rescue us. All we have to do is accept the gift.

God does not deal with us according to our goodness or blamelessness. He does not *only* show himself faithful to the faithful, or pure to the pure. He is willing to come get us where we are, as we are. "If we are faithless, he remains faithful."[xxiii]

David was correct insofar as God is happy to reward his children when they are good, but he does not simply abandon them when they are not. We have an unfair God whose jealous love chases us. He is indeed the lamp whose light we cannot outrun.

Takeaway: God's love for us is deeply unconditional.

Prayer: Lord, help me to believe that I am free because of Your love for me. Keep me from sin, but when I slip, remind me that You do not love me any less.

Greatness Within

Day 38
2 Samuel 23:8-23, 39

The retelling of David's mighty men reads like an action movie. Eleazar battled for so long that his hand literally froze to the sword he was using. Benaiah jumped into a pit and killed a lion. David's mighty three once broke the lines of a Philistine camp just to get their king a drink of water from a certain well.

The strength and courage of these warriors was incredible. These verses honor their commitment to God and to David. They also reveal two lessons.

First, we cannot get to where God wants us to go by ourselves. David discovered his destiny to be king at a young age. However, without the help of Samuel, Jonathan, these mighty men, and even Saul at times, David would have never reached his destiny.

Don't be afraid to include people in your story. When God brings people into our lives, they will not be a distraction or competitor but a companion. David was surrounded by men and women who could do things he could not so that they all could reach a higher place together.

I believe this is the lesson and attitude throughout the majority of chapter 23. It's meant to astound and encourage us. But as the memory of David's mighty men closes, it ends on a very different note.

If you read past Benaiah, through Eliphelet, and right below Gareb you will stumble across a very familiar name: Uriah the Hittite. That's right, David had one of his mighty men, one of his most loyal and famous warriors murdered so that he could hide his adultery with that man's wife.

As much as this chapter praises David and his men, it is also a stark reminder of their humanity.[xxiv]

A person who does great things is not immune to terrible mistakes. The opposite is also true. Those whose stories have been defined by great sins are not barred from great achievements.

The reality of the human condition is that each of us are capable of greatness. We must decide which path that greatness will take.

Takeaway: As long as we are alive we are still capable of great good and evil.

Prayer: Thank you God that you have made humans capable of so much. Guide my actions with your wisdom so that I do not fall down the wrong path.

David's Model of Success

Day 39
2 Samuel 24:1-25

The book of 2 Samuel ends in a seemingly strange way. After all that David had been through – all the trials and struggles and mistakes – we find in chapter 24 yet another hardship. David sins by taking a census throughout Israel which incites God to send a plague. After the plague killed a large number of people, David was able to build an altar to God and have it stopped.

This passage leaves us with so many questions. Why was a census a bad thing? What could David have done differently? And why did the author choose to end his book with this story? The answers we find will help us see the true beauty of this chapter.

First, the census David commissioned was not like the ones we experience today where every single person is counted. Instead, theirs was a military census which tracked and mobilized every "able-bodied man who could handle a sword." So why was this a bad thing?

Bible commentators go back and forth on this topic. Some believe the very act of counting the army was prideful and showed distrust in God. Regardless, David's census took Israel's focus off of God and placed it onto themselves for an extended period of time.

After the census was complete and David realized his sin, he sought God's help. God's prophet told David to go build an altar, sacrifice on it, and the plague would end. The book of 2 Samuel ends with David carrying out these directions and God stopping the plague in Israel.

This last scene encapsulates the entire message of 2 Samuel. Time and time again it seems as if God should have turned his face away from David as he did for Saul. David committed a multitude of sins just like the king he replaced. But what matters, and what is shown in this chapter, is the one thing David did differently than Saul.

David asked for God's forgiveness and acted on that forgiveness.

David trusted God because he knew he was going to fail – and he did – but David also knew that God would always pick him back up if asked.

How our failure turns out depends upon our view of God. If we see Him as loving, kind, gracious, we will run to Him like David did. If we see Him as harsh, controlling and angry, we will run the other way as Saul did.

One would think the story of David, Israel's greatest human king, should end on a high note. Instead, we see David committing a sin and asking for forgiveness. Why would his journey close this way? Because this is actually a high note – it's a final look into the element of David's life that made him truly great! David's extraordinary reign as king was a direct byproduct of his willingness to continually seek forgiveness and walk in that forgiveness.

The reason David is so important for us is because he becomes the model for how we can succeed God's way.[xxv] Trusting God shapes our view of God. A healthy view of God enables us to ask Him for forgiveness. Once we realize forgiveness is always a possibility, that is when greatness becomes a possibility.

The people of God do not succeed by always doing things the right way - that is impossible. The people of God succeed by consistently taking bold action and when they fail, they don't give up. They turn to God, ask for forgiveness, and continue to pursue God and their calling as they walk in their forgiveness.

David was a truly great king not in spite of his mistakes, but because of them. His troubles gave all of Israel the opportunity to experience the character of God.

Thousands of years later we still benefit from his ups and downs because through them we see a portrait of the God who refuses to leave us in our sin. Failure never has to be the end of our story.

Takeaway: God's forgiveness is our unfair advantage in this life.

Prayer: Lord, I want to do great things with this life you have given me. Your goodness is my foundation, your love is my calling, and your forgiveness gives me wings.

Securing the Legacy

Day 40
1 Kings 2:10-12

The finals days of David's life are captured in the first chapters of 1 Kings. David is very old now. He has reigned for approximately 40 years over all of Israel. Now his last thoughts are with his legacy. Who will take his place once he is gone? Who will guide Israel in the ways of the Lord?

There is a brief conflict between David's sons. One named Adonijah declares himself king, but he does so without the support of his father or God. All the country is curious and a number of David's officials come to ask him in person – who will you make king? That is when David makes his choice and anoints his son Solomon, the second child from Bathsheba, to be the next king of Israel.

David then dies quietly in bed. He has fulfilled his duty as king, and placed Israel in the hands of someone who will become one of the wisest men in history. David's legacy will live on.

As much as David is remembered for being king, a leader of peoples, what has stuck out most to me throughout his story is David's willingness to submit. From the shepherd fields to the palace, David never considered himself better than anyone else. He was a servant to all. A man who loved the least and fought for the weak. Above all, he kept God at the forefront of his life.

David became a king, but he never stopped seeing himself as a child of God.

My hope for myself, and for you, is that God will take us to new heights. That He will drive us to do the impossible and then show us that all things are possible in Him. Along the way, we will grow in our trust of Him.

David gained power because he cultivated trust. David acquired respect because he fostered love. David secured a legacy because he practiced forgiveness.

While David's story has ended, yours is just gaining momentum. The King of Kings waits for you – his unlikely hero, a sinner made saint. Your trust in Him will open the door.

Takeaway: The quality of our legacy depends upon what we choose to trust while living.

Prayer: Thank You Father for the gift of life. Keep my eyes on You, my trust in You, and my walk towards You.

Continuing the Journey

Thank you for reading *Crowned with David*. I hope the experience was encouraging and that you've learned just a little bit more about one of the most loved characters in the Old Testament.

Now that you've started to learn some Old Testament truths, here are two steps you can take to continue your journey.

First, sign up for my newsletter at RamosAuthor.com. There you'll receive a monthly email that contains exclusive insights, book discounts, and the free gift *Dreaming with Joseph*.

Second, please take a minute to write a short review for *Crowned with David*. These reviews help me write better, more effective books so I would deeply appreciate your support!

The one lesson from David's story that I will never forget is this: God's forgiveness is always an option. David was far from perfect, but instead of trying to hide his shortcomings he laid them openly before God. That kind of trust and transparency is the breeding ground for greatness.

I hope you will take the challenge and live a life characterized by trusting God. It will be difficult, but He is waiting to give you the crown.

About the Author

David Ramos is an author and teacher passionate about communicating the life-changing truths found in the Old Testament. He has a degree in Classical and Medieval Studies and is currently finishing a Master's in Religion (Biblical Studies) at Ashland Theological Seminary. When he's not writing you can usually find David chasing down the newest food truck or helping his fiancé Breahna plan their wedding (2016).

David and his library currently reside in Cleveland, Ohio. Visit his website at ramosauthor.com.

More Books by David Ramos

Enduring with Job: 30 Devotionals to Give You Hope, Stir Your Faith, and Find God's Power in Your Pain

Climbing with Abraham: 30 Devotionals to Help You Grow Your Faith, Build Your Life, and Discover God's Calling

Escaping with Jacob: 30 Devotionals to Help You Find Your Identity, Forgive Your Past, and Walk in Your Purpose

The God with a Plan

Twentyfive: Treasures from an Unusual Millennial Life

The Shadow of Gethsemane: An Easter Poem

Further Reading on David

David: A Man of Passion and Destiny by Charles R. Swindoll

1 & 2 Samuel from *Teach the Text Commentary Series* by Robert B. Chisholm Jr.

David: The Divided Heart by David Wolpe

Takeaway List

1. God chooses the unlikely to do great things.

2. God always delivers on His promises.

3. The life God has for us might contradict what our loved believe is best.

4. We should pursue the impossible because God's strength shows itself through our weakness.

5. In our pursuit of great callings we will have to constantly ask ourselves: am I pursuing the thing more than God.

6. The more we trust God, the more freedom we will experience in our lives.

7. God does not work in a vacuum, He uses other people for our story.

8. God's presence can either be refreshing or frightening depending on the condition of our heart.

9. We will be amazed by what happens when we let go and let God.

10. God is bigger than the big things that keep us from trusting Him.

11. Trust in God transforms us.

12. Trusting ourselves always leads to fearful living.

13. When we don't expect much from God, it's because our trust in him is small.

14. When we choose not to forgive, we are choosing to trust our own judgment over God's.

15. Our lives matter most when they are part of something bigger than ourselves.

16. God uses every kind of person to accomplish His plans.

17. God's illogical path is better than our logical one.

18. Even the best of us will fail to trust God, but He is patient.

19. Healthy communication with God goes both ways.

20. God can and does solve our problems by giving us what we do not deserve.

21. Whenever our eyes are on anything other than God, our lives will appear incomplete.

22. God will always fulfill His promise to us.

23. Trust God as much in good times as you do in bad times.

24. Every crown we achieve is both the end and beginning of our growth.

25. Evil has its role to play in this world, but God is still supreme.

26. Fearing God is part of building our trust in Him.

27. Truly great lives are directed by God.

28. God's grace, human kindness, and personal bravery make the impossible happen.

29. The simple sin of pride can lead us down a path we never imagined.

30. No matter our sin, God is standing by to forgive us and bring us back to Him.

31. Pain that is kept silent will eventually grow out of our control.

32. My pain/anger/pride does not have to define me. God is the one who defines who I truly am.

33. Trusting God and taking action are not opposing options. They can work together when we are humble.

34. An answered prayer will sometimes be accompanied by a loss.

35. Our priority must be following God rather than following rules.

36. Our sins can have bigger consequences than we know.

37. God's love for us is deeply unconditional.

38. As long as we are alive we are still capable of great good and evil.

39. God's forgiveness is our unfair advantage in this life.

40. The quality of our legacy depends upon what we choose to trust while living.

Endnotes

i Daniel 2:21

ii P. Kyle McCarter Jr., *1 Samuel* from *The Anchor Bible* (Garden City: Doubleday & Company, 1980), 297.

iii 1 Corinthians 1:27

iv McCarter Jr., 313-314.

v Ibid., 317.

vi Ibid., 329.

vii Ibid., 350.

viii Ibid., 371.

ix Daniel Bodi., *The Story of Samuel, Saul, and David* in *Ancient Israel's History: An Introduction to Issues and Sources* (Grand Rapids: Baker Academic, 2014), 220.

x Ibid., 416.

xi Ibid., 422.

xii Robert B. Chisholm Jr., *1 & 2 Samuel* from *Teach the Text Commentary Series* (Grand Rapids: Baker Books, 2013), 186.

xiii McCarter Jr., 443.

xiv Chisholm Jr., 197.

xv A.A. Anderson, *2 Samuel,* vol. 11 of *Word Biblical Commentary* (Dallas: Word Books, 1989), 22.

[xvi] Ibid., 47.
[xvii] http://biblehub.com/hebrew/4648.htm
[xviii] Anderson, 180.
[xix] Ibid., 208.
[xx] Ibid., 225.
[xxi] Ibid., 242.
[xxii] Chisholm Jr., 290.
[xxiii] 2 Timothy 2:13a
[xxiv] Anderson, 278.
[xxv] Ibid., 287.